EXPRESS YOURSELF YOGA

A Guide to Kinepathics

Anita DeFrancesco, MA

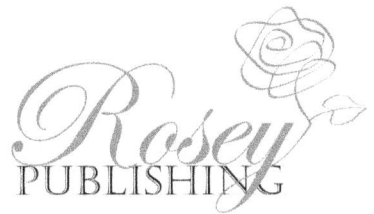

© 2004 Anita DeFrancesco, MA - All rights reserved
Reprint edition © 2023 Anita DeFrancesco, MA – All rights reserved
Printed in the United States of America

No part of this publication may be reproduced, distributed or transmitted in any form or by any means, including photocopying, recording or other electronic or mechanical methods, or by any information storage or retrieval system, without prior written permission from the publisher and/or author, except for brief quotations embodied in critical reviews and certain other non-commercial uses permitted by copyright law. For permission requests, write to author, addresses "Attention: Permissions Coordinator," at the address below.

KINEPATHICS published by:
ROSEY PUBLISHING
P.O. Box 2431
Philadelphia, Pa. 19147
anita@kinepathics.com

Photography : Nick Carrino, Philadelphia, Pa.

Front Cover Photo: Luciana LoPresto, Los Angeles, Ca.
& Dave Smith, Chicago, Il.

Backcover Photo: Mitchell Rose, Los Angeles, Ca.

Cover & Interior Design: Lori Tusiano, Bristol, Pa.
(ltusiano@comcast.net)

Creative Input: Francois Favre, JD, Los Angeles, Ca.

Director/Producer: Randolph Pitts, Lumière Films, Los Angeles, Ca.

ISBN 978-0-9822616-5-1 Trade Paperback

"The Kinepathics Method is a wonderful alternative to other forms of medical treatment."
Ron Portadin, M.D.
Vineland, NJ

MEDICAL DISCLAIMER: Not all exercises are suitable for everyone. To reduce the risk of injury do only what feels right, avoid forcing the body against its will. If you have any medical challenges or diseases consult with your physician. Please consult a phsycian before starting this or any other excercise program.

CONTENTS:

What is Yoga..vi
What is Somatic Dance Movement..................vi
What is Kinepathics......................................vi
Why do Kinepathics....................................viii
Kinepathics Benefits...................................viii
The Importance of Breath............................ix
Meditation..x
Presence..1
Let's Play...3
Open Up, Open Me Up.................................5
Challenge Me...7
Take A Walk on the Wild Side......................9
Hippo Limbo..11
Strike a Pose...13
Meow...15
Push & Pull..17
Take Me Away...19
Dive In..21
Butta Bing Butta Boom...............................23
Liquid Energy..25
What Goes Up Must Come Down................27

WHAT IS YOGA

A discipline of health and fitness that originated in India over 5000 years ago. The word Yoga means union, meaning the togetherness of the body-mind-spirit thus creating balance in the relationship of the self and with others. We begin with the breath (pranayama) followed by movement. The body is a shell of which the spirit lives. It is this spirit that needs to show its presence, passion and truth. It is when spirit meets soul that we "self actualize".

WHAT IS SOMATIC DANCE MOVEMENT

At the dawn of civilization dance and movement were an expression of healing, ritual, culture, and life celebration. It is the primal nature of where the body was born and lives within its natural movement. Modern society has forced the body to live in unnatural ways, causing a split between the mind and spirit, resulting in a loss of authentic identity. Moving with feeling during yoga encourages the body to respond from its natural impulses and directs that energy to the body's primal source. It is this source that gives us the courage to let go, move and think naturally, and find the relationship to our higher self.

WHAT IS KINEPATHICS

It is a simple, fast and easy discipline of getting your body to respond to your minds needs. It is a flow system grounded in yoga and somatic dance movement. Kinepathics was born from desire, truth, and passion (thoughted motion). It derives its meaning from the Greek words Kinesis meaning bodily movement, and Pathos meaning feeling and disease. ("moving with feeling"). (ki ná path iks) Kinepathics integrates the emotional, physical and spiritual experience of the human senses; the body's messaging system. The motions create emotion, encourage elongation, and breath body coordination. It strengthens the major muscle groups and enlivens the connective tissue. The body alignment shifts through symmetry to asymmetry according to ones feeling thoughts.

The focus is not on aesthetics but rather on feeling, and **TRANSFORMATION**. Therefore anyone can do this. This dance of shifting poses blends together the integrative process of innate intelligence. This is the movement meditation a dynamic experience of your inner rhythms. The transition between moving through space and feeling teaches us to personalize and "experience the body as a sacred home" rather than objectifying its nature. The goal is to have a relationship with the self. This builds a foundation and prepares the body from the inside out not only for exercise but for life.

To do Kinepathics is to strive for the truth, to continually become a better person, to seek out your desires and to contribute to life your share. It is a discipline to help you redefine your instrument, to look at your soul and get to know who you are, "the real you". It is a study of the self, a teaching of ones inner beliefs. Kinepathics develops our authenticity, it sharpens the senses creating an awareness of higher power that can only be sought *"in the experience"*.

During the practice I encourage you to flow and dance your body, creating a diversion from the structural poses *(freedom within structure)*. Flow from your organic spiral nature going in between the symmetrical and asymmetrical worlds. The body is the primary source of love, healing, intuition, intelligence, sensation, and

PLEASURE. This book is the beginning of a series of books into that source. Have fun, breath, and always move your body.
Allow your body to heal from it's natural powers.

WHY DO KINEPATHICS

To heal and nourish disease, to be more productive in your career, and to find potential and purpose and extend life process. To improve your physical and mental strength. To increase motivation and be inspired from the joy of living.

To condition the mind into "liberation" a freedom that we all have a right to. Kinepathics is for anyone, male/female, any age who wants to experience and take their soul to the next level of multidimension.

Anyone can save themself, it begins with the body.

KINEPATHICS BENEFITS

- reduces anxiety and high blood pressure
- develops focus, clarity, center and change
- recharges potential energy
- develops endurance, spontaneity, strength
- mediates the aging process
- enhances body esteem, sexuality, intuition
- releases deep emotional and physical blockage
- regain joy and playfulness
- learn how to work with pain as a source of information
- restores muscle and joint injuries
- decreases back and postural pains

THE IMPORTANCE OF THE BREATH
(there are 2 breaths to practice and interchange)

We are born from a breath, we are conceived from breath, movement and the senses. Breath supports movement and keeps the body in its natural flow. It is something that we should not have to think about, as it comes natural to vibrate freely from ones senses. The breath allows one to direct, focus and feel the expansions, inner movements and contractions. Breath brings about awareness to the mind, keeps the spirit free and teaches the body about space, shifting and resiliency. When the breath is combined with movement it supports change within the shifting emotions. When breathing during Yoga always finish the breath cycle before switching into the next movement. This is how we begin to transform and make a connection with our thoughts.

Ujjayi Breath: (ooh-JAI-yee) Pranayama is a practice of uniting the breath with the mind. Prana is energy, the vital life force. Ayama means to stretch or expand. The body naturally creates it's own healing

> Techinique: Bring the breath awareness to the nostrils, seal the lips; then transfer this to the throat. Imagine that the breath is being drawn in and out through the throat. Inhale and exhale through the throat creating an ocean sound in the back of the throat. Continue taking slow, calm deep breaths into the lungs and belly.

Animal Breath: This breath involves breathing from the open mouth and throat. This is similar to the la maz or tarzan breath.

It involves a pulsing from the stomach and sounds within the breath exhale.

> Technique: The body is in motion for both animal breaths. Begin by puckering up the lips, pulse from the stomach, and then moving the lips in and out and blow out a wind sound. Then shift to the throat and connect that energy to the lips (as if your running and your out of breath). When panting out from the stomach and throat make sounds from the throat, such as HA-HE-HO with incremental pauses and belly pauses. Shape the lips in all directions. Feel the stomach (diaphragm) pulse as you breath. This breath flows through connective tissue, spinal fluid, and the muscoloskeletal system thus creating more bodily space. For a variation, breath through the nose, lips sealed, continue moving the body and making throat sounds, shape the movements of the lips in all directions.

MEDITATION

To dissolve and surrender quietly to the nature of your being, formulating a relationship with the self and the universe. Usually done in stillness but can be applied during activities. Look inside and see what you see!

#1
PRESENCE

GOAL:

The goal is to introduce yourself to yourself.

MOVEMENT:

Begin by lifting the sit bones off the floor onto 2 books or 2 blankets. Bring the heels together, lean forward, to the side, unfold and open the chest by extending an arm into the space. Keep the heels pressed together. Feel the movement rising up from the lower spine as it moves outward from the ribcage. Experience and activate the flow of your senses.

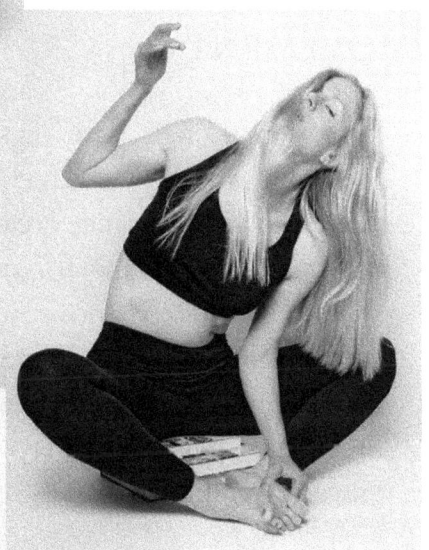

2
LETS PLAY

GOAL:

To regain playful attitude and inner environment.

MOVEMENT:

Sitting in a chair with legs folded under, first move the smile on the face, feel your sensualness, draw up from the lower spine, creating a C curve in the low back, begin thrusting forward and backward with the spine. Explore the movement! Take a tie or rope and extend it in a variety of directions that feel right to you, even hug yourself with the tie. Continue to play and breath that playful feeling way down into your tummy. Have fun! Open channels of intuitive development.

3
OPEN UP, OPEN ME UP

GOAL:

The goal is to decrease shyness, seek forth your inner nature and share that with others.

MOVEMENT:

Sit on your heels or books to help lift you. Begin to come into the energy space and thrive. Take notice of your energy, how does it want to move. Raise the hands up over the head and open your soul, then fall over forward, allow your hair to get wild, then find a new way of moving from the position, dance your way out of your inner shell. As you undo a layer, find more truth in who you really want to open up to. Breath with passion and desire.

4
CHALLENGE ME

GOAL:

To empower the edge of your being.

MOVEMENT:

Begin lying on your back and extending your legs onto the chair, lift your pelvis, stay still for 3 minutes and breath. Then begin to unfold your dance. Oblique your body, keep the pelvis lifted and begin to move from the chest and thorax. Feel the belly moving. Listen to your inner rhythms and allow the arms to sing out. Eventually drop down to the floor and continue unfolding. The movement originates from the belly and rib cage. Let the energy travel through the entire body when moving each part. Continue to challenge yourself. Keep a sense of flow as you find new direction and motion with every expression.

5
TAKE A WALK ON THE WILD SIDE

GOAL:

To breakthrough the structures that hold you back.

MOVEMENT:

Begin in a squat or frog position. Take 3 minutes of stillness and breath, then discover your wildness within. Moving through the space within the position, find new ways to unfold and move out of the structured feeling. Move the neck, energy moving upward from the tail bone area. Eventually find your way up, moving slowly vertebra by vertebra. Let go of control within your dance.

6
HIPPO LIMBO

GOAL:

To strike a balance.

MOVEMENT:

Lie on either side and take 3 minutes in stillness. After you've engaged the impulse, begin to move it out, bring your thoughts into motion. Connect to the feeling space. Shift densities and align your soul. Bringing consciousness to your feeling space and spirit. Keep shifting side to side with and without feet together. Find a balance and hang out.

7
STRIKE A POSE

GOAL:

To continually adapt and adjust to new environments

MOVEMENT:

Take the chair and strike poses going in between stillness and fluid movement. Keep the motion changing. Moving the energy throughout the whole body while shaping the integrity of your soul. Shape and experience your intuitive voice. Find a gaze with the eyes for 30 second periods, then shift directions.

8
MEOW

GOAL:

To shape your essence.

MOVEMENT:

Find your animal, find a beginning, middle and ending point and go into stillness. Engage the movement within the movement. Hover and listen for the next impulse and move it through. Unfold your energy from your spine down into your arms. Keep the fluid motion flowing around the heart, liver and kidneys.

9
PUSH & PULL

GOAL:

To flex and extend the spinal interspaces, spinal breath infusion.

MOVEMENT:

Begin sitting at the edge of the chair and reach for the stars by extending those arms, then bring it in placing the hands on the upper legs, take a moment and breath. Unfold and open out to the side expanding your rib cage, keeping the hips stable. Take it from side to side creating variations with your hands up and out or to the floor. Play with the arcs of curves while flexing and extending your spine. Retreat into dropping your head down to the floor.

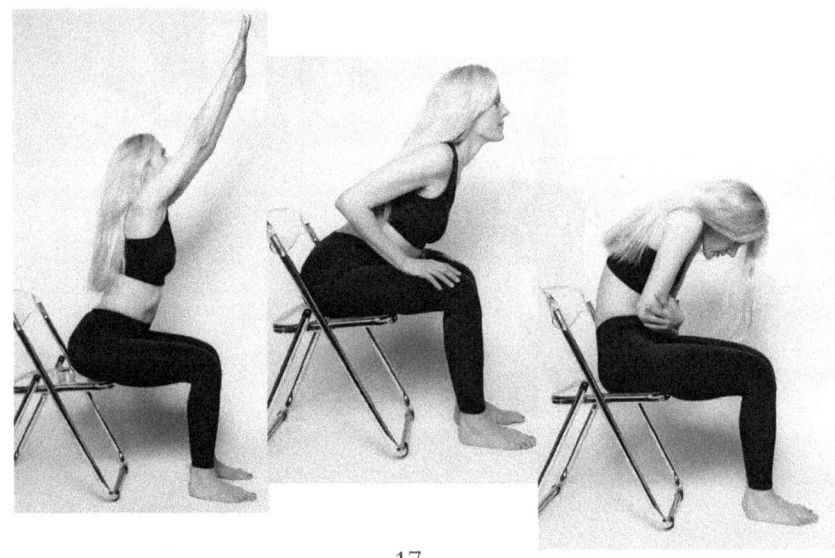

10

TAKE ME AWAY

GOAL:

To encourage and empower your spirituality.

MOVEMENT:

Sitting with your legs lengthened and or arms at the back of the chair begin to breath and create variation. Imagine that the wind is beneath you and allowing your inner self to fly taking your arms out side to side, extending forward, backward maintaining that core center. Lying on your stomach lengthen through your spine, extend through your legs and take yourself to a place that makes you happy.

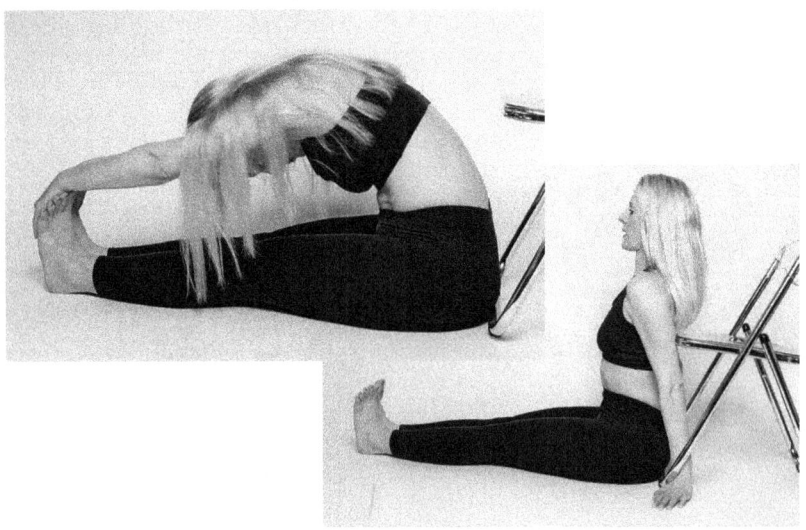

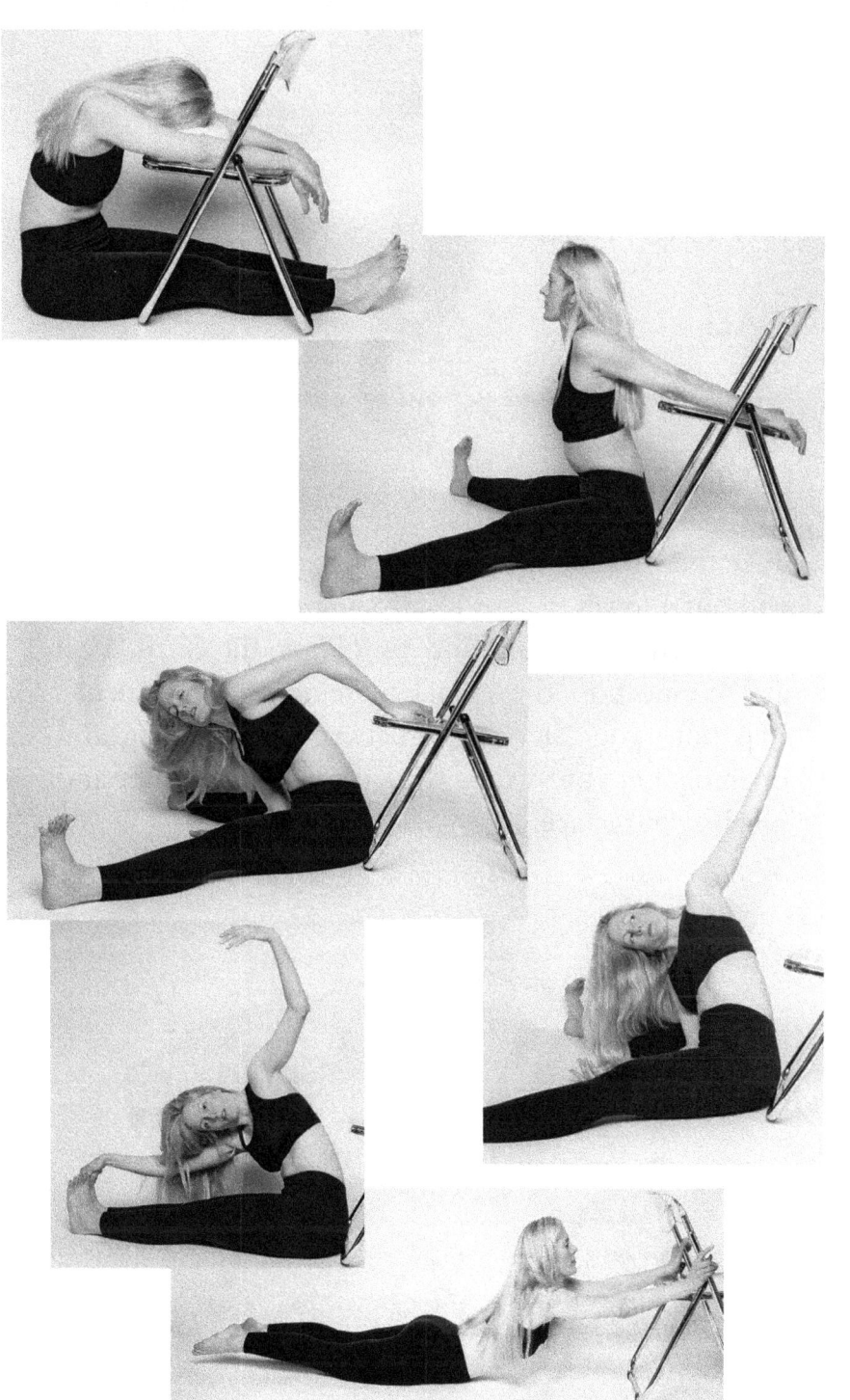

11
DIVE IN

GOAL:

To let go and get out of your own way.

MOVEMENT:

Take this inversion, extend through your spine with or without a towel at your lower spine, and open up. Go inbetween containing and unfolding the arms. Feel and connect to the spinal incremental movements. Flip onto your side go in-between lengthening and opening. Let your wings fly. Keeping your center and inhabit your space.

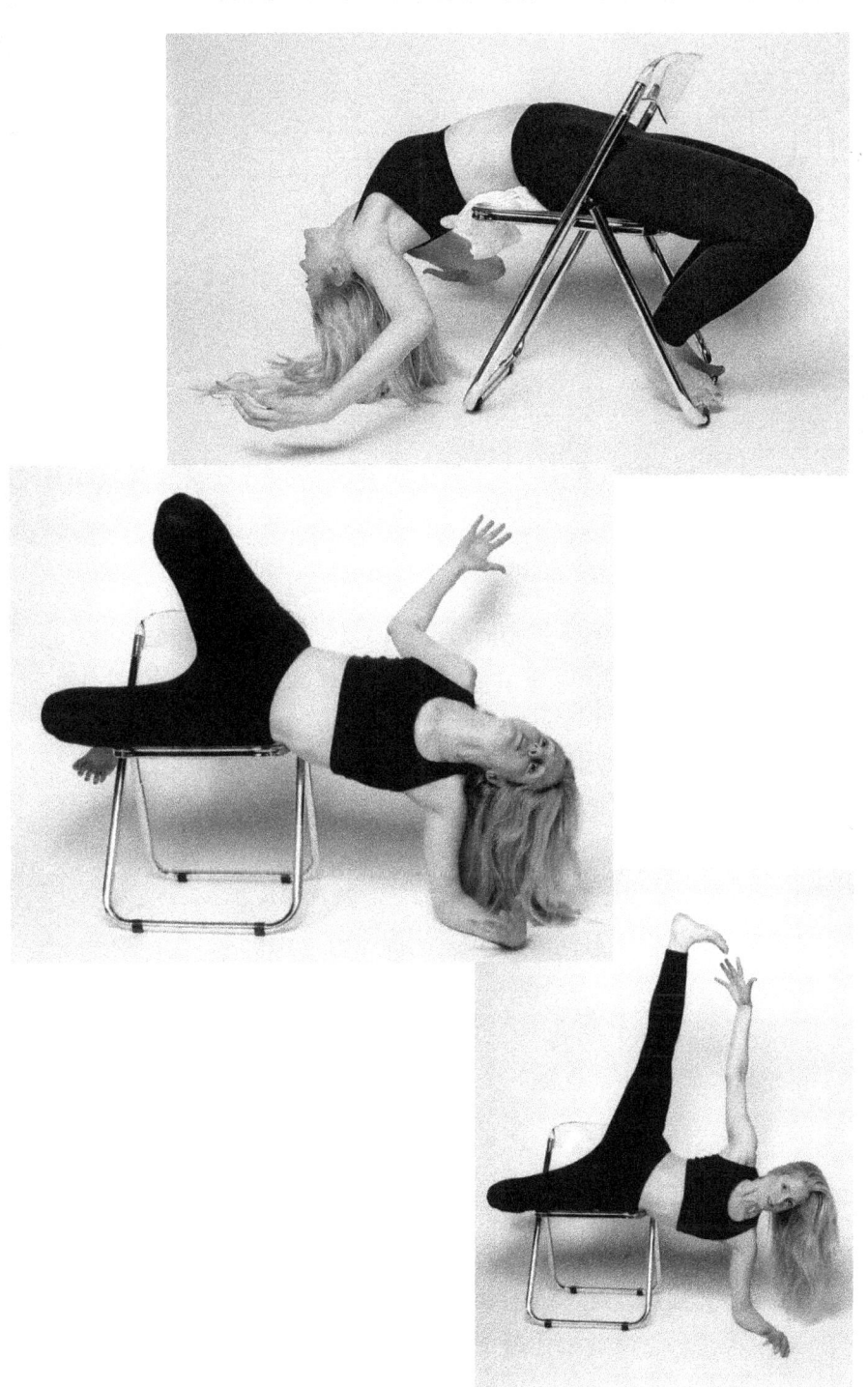

#12
BUTTA BING BUTTA BOOM

GOAL:

Interact, defend and manage your truth.

MOVEMENT:

Come into a semi-shoulder stand. Bring the knees into the face in a stillness and breath for 2 minutes. Reach your higher power by letting the legs extend and then fluidly moving them into space. Dance your soul. Stay with this for about 5 minutes. Taking it down a level, lie on your back, engaging the stomach muscles, pull forward, contract, and harness your power. Push and Pull with the gravity. Shimmy off to the sides engaging new activity.

13
LIQUID ENERGY

GOAL:

To flow and deal with truth, confidence and receptiveness.

MOVEMENT:

Take a seat and lengthen up from the lower spine, open your legs wide and feel your feet on the earth. Stay here for 3 minutes and breath. Sitting on the back sit bones maintain your balance and take both hands to the feet and spread legs into the air. Explore the passion, calmness and inner energy. For a variation take incremental steps and cross one leg over the other opening the hips. Then bring the legs together in a frog pose. Lets take an inversion, bring your legs into the air and letting go, let your head free-fall over to the floor. Keep the stomach engaged the whole time. Lastly hug both legs inward and meditate for 2 minutes.

14
WHAT GOES UP MUST COME DOWN

GOAL:

To be free, independent, contained, Stimulate emotional response and creative thought process.

MOVEMENT:

Take that chair and engage your creativeness, let your body go, advance your thoughts. Sit forward and backward and extend and flex through the spine. Lengthen through the spine and breath in and out. Fall forward over and lengthen through the legs. For creative variety lengthen the legs with a tie. When diving and flexing forward extend through the crown or head chakra. Open the neck and allow the inner spaces to adapt and flow. Add micro fluid motions to the inner neck. Let go!

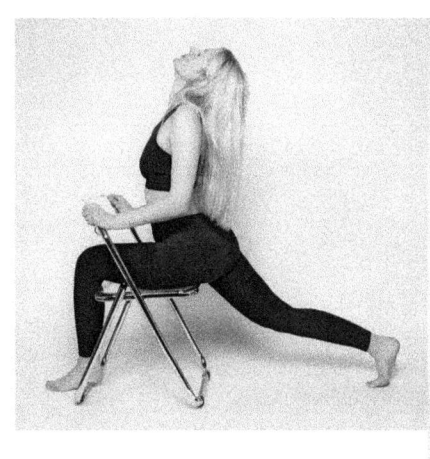
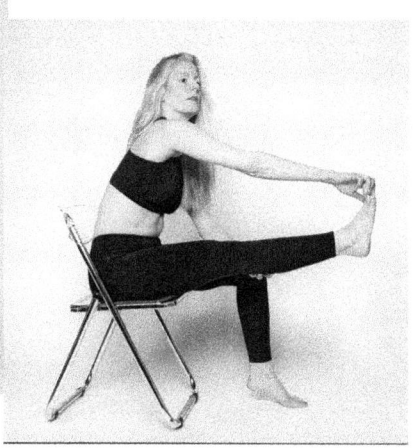

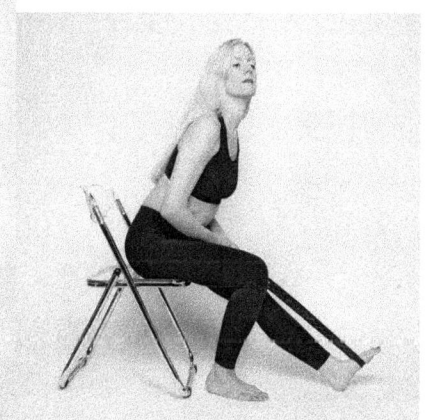
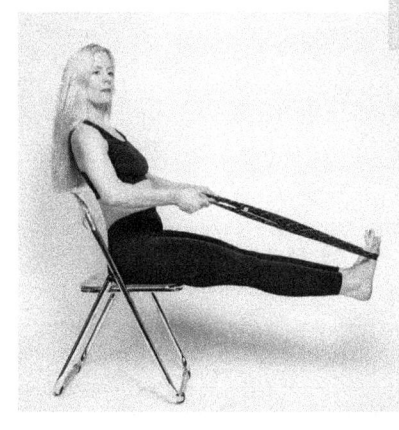

Available at amazon amazon kindle IngramSpark

Anita DeFrancesco MA, E-RYT, E-RYS, LMT

Anita is a global author, public speaker, dance movement artist, actress, somatic orgonomy psychotherapist, love and relationship coach. Holds a Master of Arts degree in Psychology and is an active member of SAG/AFTRA. A 500 hour yoga alliance registered teacher is the founder of Kinepathics and Tantra Wisdom. Author of "Live Free" "The Donna Gentile Story", and "Love Buzz". Podcast: Discover Joyous Love. A visionary leader with an insightful wisdom in the areas of self empowerment, self discovery, transformation, spirituality. A devotee of the human condition, emotional awareness, sexuality and relationships, known for her unique talents of openness, expression, and liberation. She offers classes on bonded relationships based on love, connection and consciousness. Currently living in Philadelphia is also a resident of Los Angeles. She offers workshops and teacher training programs.

www.TantraWisdom.com
www.Kinepathics.com
www.AnitaDeFrancesco.com

anita@kinepathics.com
310-210-1464

Follow her: DISCOVER JOYOUS LOVE Podcast

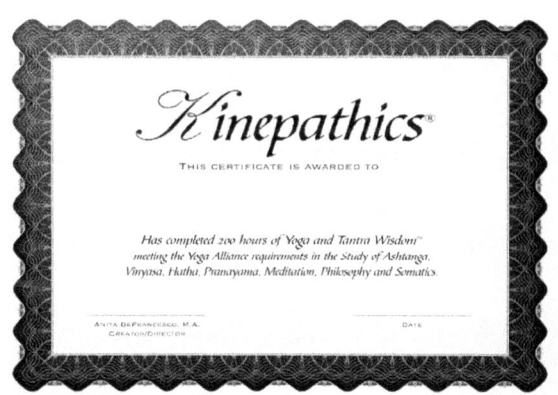

www.ingramcontent.com/pod-product-compliance
Lightning Source LLC
Chambersburg PA
CBHW071316110426
42743CB00042B/2694